GRATITUDE IS

GRATITUDE IS

The Poem & Lighthearted Empowerment Keys to Feeling Grateful

MACARENA LUZ BIANCHI

Spark Social, Inc.

Gratitude Is: The Poem & Lighthearted Keys to Feeling Grateful
ISBN: 978-1-7361801-2-9
Ebook: 978-1-7361801-3-6

Subscribe to the email list for this book spark.fyi/gpoem

First Printing, 2020 | Poem, 2006
Gratitude Is Series

Copyright © 2020 by Macarena Luz Bianchi
macarenaluzb.com

Spark Social, Inc. Miami, FL USA sparksociapress.com

All rights reserved. No part of this book may be reproduced in any manner whatsoever without written permission except in the case of brief quotations embodied in critical articles and reviews.

Contents

Dedication vi

The Poem Begins 1

The Full Poem 43

About Gratitude 47
About the Author 49

In appreciation of you.

The Poem Begins

Gratitude is... appreciation for people, places, and things, as well as, for ideas, qualities, and feelings

Gratitude is thankfulness, and I use it as a key

A key to inspiring strangers, my friends, and me

A key to life that sets me free

A key to healing insult and injury

Gratitude unlocks awareness when I refuse to dream

A key to finding forgiveness and feeling peace

A key to manifest my desires, what I wish, and whom I want to be

A key to light the dark times, when I can't see

Gratitude expresses my preferences, what I love, the real me

A key to feeling the present moment, gently

A key to reconnect me to humility

A key to boundless opportunity, when I get caught in my limited certainty

Gratitude unlocks transcendence, imagination, and epiphany

A key to turn the hardest moment into a glorious journey

A key to the only foolproof-system of love in the galaxy

A key to access infinite possibilities

When I share my gratitude, gratitude enriches you and me

Gratitude is... actually the doorway, CHOICE is the real key, so when in doubt, Gratitude is the best choice for you and me

And, the best part about gratitude is... that gratitude is always, absolutely, free!

The Full Poem

Gratitude Is

Gratitude is... appreciation for people, places, and things, as well as, for ideas, qualities, and feelings

Gratitude is thankfulness, and I use it as a key
- A key to inspiring strangers, my friends, and me
- A key to life that sets me free
- A key to healing insult and injury

Gratitude unlocks awareness when I refuse to dream
- A key to finding forgiveness and feeling peace
- A key to manifest my desires, what I wish, and whom I want to be
- A key to light the dark times, when I can't see

Gratitude expresses my preferences, what I love, the real me
- A key to feeling the present moment, gently
- A key to reconnect me to humility
- A key to boundless opportunity, when I get caught in my limited certainty

Gratitude unlocks transcendence, imagination, and epiphany
- A key to turn the hardest moment into a glorious journey
- A key to the only foolproof-system of love in the galaxy
- A key to access infinite possibilities

When I share my gratitude, gratitude enriches you and me

Gratitude is... actually the doorway, CHOICE is the real key, so when in doubt, Gratitude is the best choice for you and me

And, the best part about gratitude is... that gratitude is always, absolutely, free!

About Gratitude

Thank you for getting this coloring book! You can join the email list for it at spark.fyi/gpoem. If you like this, please leave a review on Amazon.

I wrote this poem to capture the magical and empowering potential of implementing the simple metaphysical tool of being grateful. My *Gratitude Is* series includes a color gift book to vibrant flowers, a journal, coloring book, and kids' book introducing Gift, Gilbert, and Gail, the Grateful Giraffes. You can find these and gratitude goodies at macarenaluzbianchi.com/series/gratitude. Subscribe to the email list for this book spark.fyi/gpoem.

In 2006, I started playing the Gratitude Game daily with my dear friend J.J. We wanted to support each other. Playing also provided a delightful way to stay connected during my travels. We left phone messages each other messages each day, declaring what we were grateful for. I would state things like "I appreciate the sun is shining! I appreciate I love my magical life! I appreciate I get to see my stepsons today..." on and on.

This simple ritual transformed my life. It was like magic. In a short time, it reprogrammed my brain to look at the positive in all situations. When I didn't feel right, I appreciated the relaxation opportunity being under the weather created. When something went wrong, I appreciated the solution, whether or not I knew what it was—making gratitude a habit in this way made me a better problem solver by setting me on a grateful solution-oriented path. It also made me much more fun to be around. My default state became a steady flow of thankfulness. Today, I have to be careful not to start voicemails with, "I appreciate..." and remember that I don't have to play with every call I make. Gratitude can do this and much more for you.

In my courses and private practice, I help my students and clients access their glory through wonder, wellness, and wisdom. Gratitude is a unique superpower tool that is all three: wonder, wellness, and wisdom. Therefore, gratitude is one of my favorite supporters of glorious living because it is also the pathway to achieving it, and all you may desire in life.

About the Author

Macarena Luz Bianchi is a personal development coach and holistic practitioner. She's kindly known as a Fairy Godmother to her clients. Her lighthearted empowerment approach helps people tap into their glory through wonder, wellness, and wisdom.

She created the Awaken the Wizard Within material and courses to teach simple yet powerful metaphysical tools. She has found problems, imbalances, and dissatisfaction with life arise when people ignore their energetic side. Her nondenominational sensibility stems from growing up atheist in Catholic cultures. She noticed individuals who displaced responsibility on external factors were disempowered.

She specializes in self-esteem building. She can see how individuals program themselves for disempowerment because she's done her inner work and helped her clients build consistent and sustainable confidence. The Hot Project is her makeover-system that strengthens an individual's confidence foundation so their self-esteem can blossom from the inside out.

She writes fiction and non-fiction for children and adults.

Originally from Santiago, Chile, she lives in Miami, Florida, and online at macarenaluzb.com, where you can sign up for her newsletter, download gratefulness development freebies, and explore her Lighthearted Empowerment Academy.

Macarena Luz Bianchi's
LIGHTHEARTED EMPOWERMENT ACADEMY

MEMBERSHIP CLUBS

The Hot Project Club is a monthly Self-Esteem Makeover from the Inside Out

BOOKS

Gratitude Is Series

- *Gratitude Is: A Lighthearted Empowerment Poem* Gift Book
- *Gratitude Is: Poem & Coloring Book*
- *The Grateful Giraffes: What is Gratitude?* Children's Book

Awaken the Wizard Within Series

- Level I: *Muscle Testing & Biofeedback for Muggles: Awaken the Wizard Within 101*
- Level II: *More Magic for Awakened Wizards: Awaken the Wizard Within 1002*
- Level II: *Enchanting Practice for Awakened Wizards: Awaken the Wizard Within 1003 Workbook*

The Hot Project Series

- Yes, You're Hot! The Step-by-Step Guide to Sizzling Self-Esteem Inside and Out

Your Fairy Godmother's Guide to Life Series

RaveAlone! A Coming of Age Story: The Screenplay & Production Notes

ONLINE COURSES

Awaken the Wizard Within | Level I

- 101 Biofeedback & Muscle Testing for Muggles
- 102 Light's Counterpart to Negativity - Energy Management & Alignment
- 103 Glorious Living with Wonder, Wellness & Wisdom - Energy Management

Awaken the Wizard Within | Level II

- 1001 Higher Self Consulting & Akashic Records Reading
- 1002 More Magic for Awakened Wizards
- 1003 Enchanting Practice for Awakened Wizards

Awaken the Wizard Within | Level III

- 2001 Higher Self Consulting & Reading the Akashic Records for Others

Awaken the Wizard Within | Level IV

- 3001 Teaching Higher Self Consulting

www.ingramcontent.com/pod-product-compliance
Lightning Source LLC
Chambersburg PA
CBHW030916080526
44589CB00010B/337